BY SUNNY HAPPY KIDS

WOULD YOU RATHER FOR TEENS

The Book of Silly Scenarios, Challenging Choices and Hilarious Situations Your Friends and Family Will Love!

WOULD YOU RATHER

get dumped via text message
~OR~
in front of all your friends?

be popular among your
schoolmates
~OR~
be popular among your
teachers?

WOULD YOU RATHER

your parents adopted another child

~OR~

find out you were adopted?

be freaking cool

~OR~

be super hot? (physically)

WOULD YOU RATHER

lie to your crush
~OR~
lie to your best friend?

watch your crush get
embarrassed in public
~OR~
be embarrassed in the presence
of your crush?

WOULD YOU RATHER

share your room with your
sibling
~OR~
move into the attic?

shop at a vintage store
~OR~
at Chanel?

WOULD YOU RATHER

wear a uniform to school
~OR~
wear casual outfits to school?

go to the library
~OR~
download electronic books
online?

WOULD YOU RATHER

get a pet dog
~OR~
a pet cat?

miss prom
~OR~
miss graduation?

WOULD YOU RATHER

listen to Hip hop
~OR~
rap music?

have extra lessons at school
~OR~
a private lesson teacher at home?

WOULD YOU RATHER

go to summer school
~OR~
math camp?

have a birthday party at home
~OR~
go out with friends on your birthday?

WOULD YOU RATHER

rather stream movies
~OR~
download movies?

eat an entire pack of Oreos
~OR~
a bottle of Pringles?

WOULD YOU RATHER

pack your lunch from home
~OR~
eat cafeteria food?

be driven to school
~OR~
have to take the public bus to school?

WOULD YOU RATHER

learn how to write songs
~OR~
learn how to sing?

be in a ballet class
~OR~
a salsa class?

WOULD YOU RATHER

watch a football game
~OR~
a basketball game?

wear sneakers to school
~OR~
wear shoes to school?

WOULD YOU RATHER

be a fast writer
~OR~
a fast reader?

listen to music with headphones
~OR~
earphones?

WOULD YOU RATHER

spend the weekend indoors
~OR~
outdoors?

go to a picnic
~OR~
a cook-out?

WOULD YOU RATHER

eat something grilled
~OR~
something roasted?

go to a pool party
~OR~
a beach party?

WOULD YOU RATHER

jog around
~OR~
take a stroll?

stay up all night
~OR~
stay in bed all day?

WOULD YOU RATHER

watch a tragedy movie
~OR~
a comedy?

have popular older siblings
~OR~
older siblings who are greatly feared?

WOULD YOU RATHER

travel by road

~OR~

by air?

spend your holidays at your grandma's place

~OR~

your cousin's?

WOULD YOU RATHER

be the first child

~OR~

the last child?

be an only child

~OR~

have lots of siblings?

WOULD YOU RATHER

be popular only on social media
~OR~
be popular in real life?

have your own car
~OR~
your own house?

WOULD YOU RATHER

have your phone taken away
~OR~
your laptop taken away?

it was winter all the time
~OR~
it was summer all the time?

WOULD YOU RATHER

have blue eyes
~OR~
brown eyes?

curl your hair
~OR~
dye your hair?

WOULD YOU RATHER

visit a museum
~OR~
an art gallery?

have a big bed
~OR~
a big bedroom?

WOULD YOU RATHER

wear leather clothing
~OR~
cotton clothing?

have a pool
~OR~
a jacuzzi?

WOULD YOU RATHER

cook dinner

~OR~

wash the dishes after dinner?

go to McDonald's

~OR~

Domino's?

WOULD YOU RATHER

act as the villain in a movie
~OR~
be the hero?

meet a famous movie star
~OR~
a famous musician?

WOULD YOU RATHER

be able to walk through doors
~OR~
be able to teleport?

gossip
~OR~
be gossiped about?

WOULD YOU RATHER

surf the internet
~OR~
surf the ocean?

be out when it's raining
~OR~
when it's really sunny?

WOULD YOU RATHER

get chocolates
~OR~
get candies?

wash the dirty laundry
~OR~
fold up the clothes?

WOULD YOU RATHER

have a maid

~OR~

a chef?

take a group picture with your friends

~OR~

a group selfie?

WOULD YOU RATHER

visit the optician
~OR~
visit the dentist?

take a shower
~OR~
take a bath?

WOULD YOU RATHER

wash the toilets
~OR~
wash the bathrooms?

eat a cake
~OR~
eat a pie?

WOULD YOU RATHER

be an adult already
~OR~
be a child again?

date a really smart geek
~OR~
a talented jock?

WOULD YOU RATHER

lend money from your sibling
~OR~
from your friend?

work part-time at a clothing store
~OR~
a bookstore?

WOULD YOU RATHER

watch over your younger sibling
at home
~OR~
take your younger sibling out?

use an iPhone
~OR~
a Samsung?

WOULD YOU RATHER

go dancing
~OR~
watch people dance?

be alone when sick
~OR~
have a lot of friends around?

WOULD YOU RATHER

be at the top of your class academically

~OR~

top of your team in sports?

eat in bed

~OR~

in front of the TV?

WOULD YOU RATHER

eat a bowl of ice-cream
~OR~
drink a cup of hot chocolate?

have celebrity parents
~OR~
celebrity friends?

WOULD YOU RATHER

learn how to cook
~OR~
learn how to bake?

watch a reality show
~OR~
be on a reality show?

WOULD YOU RATHER

have a lot of followers on Twitter
~OR~
on Instagram?

be Prom King/Queen
~OR~
class Valedictorian?

WOULD YOU RATHER

have loud neighbors
~OR~
really quiet neighbors?

have a skateboard
~OR~
a hover-board?

WOULD YOU RATHER

win a sports car
~OR~
win a bike?

be really tall
~OR~
really short?

WOULD YOU RATHER

ride on a horse's back

~OR~

a camel's back?

be in a quiz competition

~OR~

in a debate competition?

WOULD YOU RATHER

eat only vegetables for a month
~OR~
eat only fruits for a month?

drink tea
~OR~
drink orange juice during breakfast?

WOULD YOU RATHER

have a casual birthday party
~OR~
a theme birthday party?

how to play the piano
~OR~
know how to play the guitar?

WOULD YOU RATHER

go fishing
~OR~
go hunting?

be in a day school
~OR~
a boarding school?

WOULD YOU RATHER

have a lot of money
~OR~
be good looking?

have a male best friend
~OR~
a female best friend?

WOULD YOU RATHER

spend your afternoon reading
your notes
~OR~
reading a magazine?

have a best friend who's an
introvert
~OR~
one who's an extrovert?

WOULD YOU RATHER

go to a music concert

~OR~

watch MTV Base?

know how to swim

~OR~

know how to surf?

WOULD YOU RATHER

meet your mentor
~OR~
your celebrity crush?

be in a relationship with
someone far away
~OR~
someone in your class?

WOULD YOU RATHER

get a follow from Barrack
Obama on Twitter
~OR~
Kanye West?

dress fashionably
~OR~
comfortably?

WOULD YOU RATHER

be popular at school
~OR~
date someone popular?

win a gift card
~OR~
win cash?

WOULD YOU RATHER

have a babysitter
~OR~
be forced to babysit?

burn your uniform while ironing
~OR~
tear your uniform while washing?

WOULD YOU RATHER

watch a scary movie at night
~OR~
a scary movie when you're
home alone for the weekend?

have really large feet
~OR~
really large hands?

WOULD YOU RATHER

constantly sneeze
~OR~
constantly itch?

lose 10 friends
~OR~
gain 5 enemies?

WOULD YOU RATHER

have a weird smile
~OR~
a weird laugh?

have a monkey that talks
~OR~
a monkey that dances?

WOULD YOU RATHER

have all your teeth fall out
~OR~
all your hair fall out?

hop around
~OR~
walk backward?

WOULD YOU RATHER

have your head attached
backward
~OR~
your eyes at the back of your
head?

prank your parents
~OR~
have your parents try to prank
you?

WOULD YOU RATHER

kiss a frog

~OR~

hug a skunk?

swallow gum accidentally

~OR~

have it stuck in your hair?

WOULD YOU RATHER

be chased by a hobo
~OR~
a hobo's dog?

your younger sister did your homework
~OR~
you did your younger sister's homework?

WOULD YOU RATHER

have all your teeth fall out
~OR~
have two tongues?

have really bushy eyebrows
~OR~
no eyebrows at all?

WOULD YOU RATHER

have a friend that smells weird
~OR~
a friend that acts weird?

your dog pooped on your
homework
~OR~
your dog ate your homework?

WOULD YOU RATHER

have a pimple on your nose
~OR~
in between your eyes?

pour your lunch on the principal
~OR~
the most popular person in school?

WOULD YOU RATHER

fart loudly in class
~OR~
in the hallway?

walk into baby poop
~OR~
dog poop?

WOULD YOU RATHER

walk around with something
taped to your back
~OR~
stuck in your hair?

drink something that'll give you a
pink tongue
~OR~
a black tongue?

WOULD YOU RATHER

be really hairy all over
~OR~
have a bald head?

have a big head
~OR~
a long neck?

WOULD YOU RATHER

have a crooked voice
~OR~
a squeaky voice?

have a friend who reveals too
much personal information
~OR~
who doesn't know how to keep
secrets?

WOULD YOU RATHER

win in a pie eating contest
~OR~
in a drinking contest?

be caught singing in the
bathroom loudly
~OR~
talking to yourself in the mirror?

WOULD YOU RATHER

be a terrible dancer

~OR~

be a terrible singer?

have an embarrassing picture of
you circulate around school

~OR~

circulate on the internet?

WOULD YOU RATHER

your mom dressed funny to school

~OR~

brought your baby pictures to show your classmates?

be in college already

~OR~

go back to Kindergarten?

WOULD YOU RATHER

have parents who dress like teenagers

~OR~

parents who dress like grandparents?

not be able to hear anything while watching TV

~OR~

not be able to see anything?

WOULD YOU RATHER

sit on something wet

~OR~

sit on something sticky?

date someone goofy

~OR~

date someone weird?

WOULD YOU RATHER

have a long nose

~OR~

a fat nose?

have a wide face

~OR~

a long face?

WOULD YOU RATHER

be able to land on the sun
~OR~
live alone in Pluto?

be tickled
~OR~
tickle someone?

WOULD YOU RATHER

have tentacles for hands
~OR~
legs?

wear your clothes inside out
~OR~
backward?

WOULD YOU RATHER

have to wear a clown nose

~OR~

a clown wig everywhere you go?

have milk squirt out of your nose

~OR~

out of your ears?

WOULD YOU RATHER

always laugh at sad things
~OR~
always cry at funny things?

find out Santa Claus was real
~OR~
Tooth Fairies were real?

WOULD YOU RATHER

fall asleep on a public bus
~OR~
in class?

laugh so hard you started to cry
~OR~
laugh so hard you couldn't breathe?

81

WOULD YOU RATHER

drink and eat from a baby
feeding bottle

~OR~

never eat in public again?

eat the family pet

~OR~

not eat for a week?

WOULD YOU RATHER

have wings
~OR~
have a tail?

use someone else's toothbrush
~OR~
find out someone used your toothbrush?

WOULD YOU RATHER

be abducted by Zombies

~OR~

Aliens?

have your face painted while
you were asleep

~OR~

have your tummy painted?

WOULD YOU RATHER

wake up with a new face
~OR~
wake up to see a new family?

meet a mini you
~OR~
an evil version of you?

WOULD YOU RATHER

dump your lunch tray on the
school bully

~OR~

on your Hall monitor?

prank your neighbor

~OR~

stalk your neighbor?

WOULD YOU RATHER

have to sing with a terrible voice in public

~OR~

have to dance offbeat in public?

wear oversized clothes to school

~OR~

clothes that are much too small?

WOULD YOU RATHER

fall asleep for a year
~OR~
have insomnia for a year?

have a fat tummy
~OR~
fat cheeks?

WOULD YOU RATHER

have gap teeth
~OR~
have to use braces for your teeth?

have six fingers
~OR~
six toes?

WOULD YOU RATHER

sweat from your nose
~OR~
sweat from your ears?

be ridiculously tiny
~OR~
be ridiculously huge?

WOULD YOU RATHER

be trapped in a room full of talking dolls

~OR~

walking teddy bears?

have your mom kiss your cheeks in public

~OR~

call you your childhood nickname in public?

WOULD YOU RATHER

fall off a bike

~OR~

fall off a skateboard?

be terrible at cooking

~OR~

be terrible at baking?

WOULD YOU RATHER

still cuddle with stuffed animals
at night
~OR~
talk to stuffed animals at night?

be so tired your mom had to
bath you
~OR~
be so tired your best friend had
to bath you?

WOULD YOU RATHER

wake up to find your hair bald
~OR~
to find out that your hair turned pink?

your friend uploaded a picture where your outfit looked weird
~OR~
your face looked weird?

WOULD YOU RATHER

walk into the wrong class
~OR~
carry the wrong notes to school?

walk around after a shower with
soap in your hair
~OR~
soap behind your ears?

WOULD YOU RATHER

fall into a swimming pool
~OR~
fall into a pool of water?

be involved in a food fight
~OR~
start a pillow fight?

WOULD YOU RATHER

your best friend dressed like someone from the 80's

~OR~

someone from another planet entirely?

be dumped in front of the whole school

~OR~

be dumped on a live video online?

WOULD YOU RATHER

work as a clown
~OR~
work in a circus?

have weird siblings
~OR~
have weird friends?

WOULD YOU RATHER

chase a crawling cockroach
~OR~
be chased by a flying cockroach?

have a childish older sibling
~OR~
a younger sibling that likes to boss you around?

WOULD YOU RATHER

have parents that looked like young people
~OR~
parents that dressed like young people?

be pursued by chickens
~OR~
be pursued by turkeys?

WOULD YOU RATHER

be known as the teacher's pet in school

~OR~

be known as mummy's pet at home?

wear two different legs of socks to school

~OR~

two different legs of shoes?

WOULD YOU RATHER

snore when you sleep
~OR~
talk when you sleep?

sit in between two really fat people
~OR~
two really smelly people?

WOULD YOU RATHER

have to work on a farm after school

~OR~

have to work on a field after school?

sneeze really loud

~OR~

sneeze really hard?

Made in the USA
Monee, IL
17 December 2022

22119052R00059